Virgin ISLANDS

THOSE who travel to the Virgin Islands can anticipate all the customary delights of the Caribbean: coral reefs, silky shores, romantic hideaways and reggae rhythms. It's not uncommon to see brightly hued parakeets, pelicans and canaries, or maybe an iguana or two!

Vacationers also expect warm, balmy weather in this region. Day temperatures range in the 80s and rarely does it rain. All this is conducive to a remarkable variety of plant life, from lichen and mosses to fruit trees and orchids. The main islands of St. Thomas and St. John display an abundance of tropical foliage with St. Thomas having 1,220 different plants in its 32 square miles. St. Croix just may be the most fragrant isle with 42 varieties of orchids and almost double that amount of morning glories.

The terrain of the Virgin Islands is a marvelous mixture of rugged coasts and satiny shorelines created long ago from volcanic explosions. Some of the beaches, Magens Bay, Trunk Bay, and Hawk's Nest, are ranked among the very best. With its crystal blue water and gentle palms swaying in the breeze, this little corner of the world is a breathtaking sight to behold.

Virgin ISLANDS

WATER sports enthusiasts seem to agree that the waters of the Virgin Islands offer some of the greatest sailing, boating and fishing in the world. Both power and sail vessels are plentiful in the Caribbean to ensure its visitors get exactly the adventure they're seeking. St. Thomas is considered the charter boat hub of the Caribbean, while adjacent islands offer serene coves for sailing or anchoring. Tradewinds, wave action and warm water all contribute to an enjoyable day at sea. The range of trips by boat includes day sails, high-speed ferry rides, glass bottom boat rides and sundown cruises.

Beneath the water is a whole new world to explore. For snorkelers and scuba divers, these turquoise waters provide a glorious look at life below the sea. Beautiful and mysterious creatures of the deep feed on spectacular coral reefs of violet, yellow, orange and red. Reefs of elkhorn and brain coral are home to an entire underwater civilization including some of the most challenging sport fish anywhere. Saltwater anglers are likely to have blue marlin, wahoo, kingfish and tuna among their catch. Well-seasoned sailors and novice seafarer alike will find unlimited pleasure on and below these waters.

Saint THOMAS

T HE ever-popular Magens Bay of St. Thomas *(above left, lower left, lower right)* is surrounded by luxurious villas of the wealthy. Its world-renowned pristine beaches form a mile-long horseshoe around the bay. It is an excellent place to sink your toes in the velvety sand or take a refreshing swim in placid waters. From the top of Magens Bay lies Drake's Seat, so named for Sir Francis Drake who reportedly used this panoramic spot for his lookout.

The Morning Star Beach *(upper center)* is a very public place to which the resident population flocks on weekends. While there's little peace or privacy here, the many bars, restaurants and water sports make this a lively retreat for those seeking fun in the sun.

A breathtaking 360 degree view of marine life awaits visitors of Coral World *(upper right)*. An underwater observatory settled 20 feet below sea level affords an awesome view of the world's largest natural reef exhibit. Its Marine Garden Aquariums contain unusual species such as purple anemones and fluorescent coral. Guests are invited to pet a starfish, observe shark feeding, shop or dine at this popular attraction.

Saint THOMAS

A N eclectic mix of architecture rests on St. Thomas where the structures have withstood the influences of Danish and German settlers, French refugees, pirates, slaves and military forces. Bluebeard's Castle *(top, near left)*, a stone fortress perched above the town, was built as a watchtower at the onset of the Danish settlement on St. Thomas. The complex *(bottom, near left)* now houses a hotel and restaurants. The Grand Hotel *(top, center)*, once reserved for the social elite, also operates shops and restaurants. Hotel 1829 *(center)* is considered one of the island's most charming, and an excellent example of 19th century architecture.

Blackbeard's Tower *(bottom, center)* dates to 1679 when it served as a lookout to alert forces at Fort Christian of enemy attacks by sea. Perpendicular to the stone tower is the infamous 99 Steps *(top, far right)*, a stairway "street" comprised of yellow bricks from Denmark and red bricks from England, France and Spain.

Places of worship on St. Thomas include Saints Peter and Paul Catholic Church *(middle, far right)* and the Synagogue of Berecha V'Shalom V'Gemilath Chasidim *(bottom, far right)*, the oldest synagogue on the island and the second oldest in the western hemisphere.

Saint THOMAS

S URELY one of the most stunning views to see in St. Thomas is its capital, the town of Charlotte Amalie (*top, near left; top, center*) shown here from atop the Black-beards. Named in 1691 for the Queen of Denmark, this natural deep water port is harbor to the many vessels that grace these waters (*middle, near left; top, far right*). This includes the massive cruise liners like those docked near the Havensight Mall (*bottom, near left*).

A sightseeing tour will take you to castles, fortresses and warehouses where pirates once stashed their treasures. Find a map and stroll at your leisure or allow a local historian to provide a guided tour. Visit the Main Street corridor and you'll find pretty pastel buildings and sidewalks bustling with tourists. Though it's not a very big city, most of the 51,000 residents of St. Thomas live in Charlotte Amalie.

If you like the looks of St. Thomas by day, you'll be nothing short of enchanted by its sunsets (*middle, far right*). The warm evening sun casts a picture-perfect glow over the island. As nightfall progresses, thousands of twinkling lights luminate the ships in harbor (*bottom, right*) and shimmer across the bay.

Saint CROIX

T HE sugar cane plantations and ruins *(upper photos, near left)* may well be St. Croix's most fascinating attraction. Knowledgeable tour guides of the St. Croix Landmark Society relate stories of 18th century plantation life. Over 150 windmills circled in these parts for more than a century. Virtually every inch of soil fit for cultivating was used to grow sugar cane, which the planters revered as "gold" *(bottom, left)*. The Estate Whim sugar mill operated a Dutch-type windmill *(lower right)* and an animal mill powered by oxen, mules or horses. Once the steam engine was introduced, however, these mills were no longer used. The giant steam-powered mill required a towering chimney *(far right)* to create a draft for the engine.

The Whim Greathouse *(center)* constructed in the 1700s is an oval building nearly 100 feet long and 35 feet wide. Its neo-classical style features walls almost three feet thick built of limestone, coral and rock and coated in plaster to prevent decay. Interior furnishing are exemplary of the 1800s.

Visitors to the estate are welcome to view other points of interest such as a museum, gift shop, caretakers cottage, watch house, distillery and apothecary.

Saint CROIX

S T. CROIX, largest of the Virgin Islands, offers romantic vistas of rolling hills and gorgeous island blooms - so lush it's virtually unforgettable. The shallowness of its harbor prevents cruise ships from docking, but a fleet of yachts is always anchored at the wharfs. Across the way is the Hotel on the Cay...Protestant Cay, that is *(top, near left)*. The isle's name dates to the late 1600s when non-Catholics refused to be buried on the main island and were thus laid to rest here.

Christiansted, the larger of the two towns here, is known for its well-preserved historical sites. Jaunt over to King Street *(lower left)* if shopping strikes your fancy. This is one of the major shopping locales where hand wrought jewelry, exotic perfumes, Cruzan rum and other island specialties are available, all duty-free! Also on King Street is the Government House *(top, far right)*, landmark public building of the island.

Fort Christiansvaern *(center and bottom photos, right)* was erected by the Danes in 1774 to shield the harbor. The National Park Service manages the fort which is thought to be one of the best-preserved 18th century forts in the Caribbean.

Saint CROIX

T RAVEL back in time at Frederiksted, located on the west coast of St. Croix. In 1776, the Stars and Stripes of the newly-formed American republic was honored at Fort Frederik *(top and bottom photos, left)* for the first time. Legend has it that when the United States declared her independence, the fort fired its canons as the flag was raised. Some 72 years later at this fort, the proclamation emancipating the slaves was read. In commemorating the bicentennial, the fort was restored in 1976 and now is home to a museum.

In addition to the fort, Frederiksted has a lovely waterfront *(photos top center and lower right)* frequented by the the many vessels bound for St. Croix. This is a quiet town with colonial style *(top, far right)* as seen in its architecture. This quaint little town wasn't always so serene, though. In 1878 it was heavily burned during labor riots and most of its landmarks have since been restored. Be sure to stop by Bell House, Victoria House and Customs House, all landmarks with an old world ambience.

Saint CROIX

MAGNIFICENT lawns and flora captivate audiences at the the St. George Village Botanical Gardens *(bottom and middle, left)* on St. Croix. There's much to be admired here: delicate hibiscus, the showy pink and purple blooms of bougainvillea that sprawl across this old sugar mill *(top, left)* and brilliant red and orange petals that adorn the flambouyants. This 16-acre estate features a Crucian Rain Forest along with the restored greathouse, rum factory, baker's shop and dam of the St. George Village sugar plantation.

Guests of the Virgins will be hard-pressed to find more accommodating inns, villas and hotels than on St. Croix. The finest amenities and seaside views await at Carambola Beach Resort at Davis Bay Beach *(top, far right)*. Those who enjoy a challenge should partake in a round of golf at its lush and expertly manicured course *(top, center)*.

Likewise, the Buccaneer Hotel *(center and bottom photos, right)*, a powder pink beauty fringed with palm trees, offers golf and tennis facilities with an ocean of blue as a backdrop. After a day of sporting here, consider indulging in a meal of sumptuous island cuisine served in the elegant banquet room.

Saint CROIX

HE easternmost point of St. Croix is at Point Udall where cactus and other succulents thrive in the warm, dry climate *(top and bottom, near left)*. When Christopher Columbus sailed his second voyage in 1493, Point Udall is the part of the Virgin Islands he sighted first.

Trek down a seaside path to a white sand beach and inviting blue-green waters at Grapetree Bay *(top, right)*. Graceful palms and seagrape trees will be swaying to a constant tropical breeze.

The coral reefs off Buck Island *(right, center)* are a nature lover's dream. Sailboats and power cruisers deliver the adventuresome to this isle. Once below the water, marked trails guide snorkelers and divers to some of the most prolific coral in the Caribbean. Spectacular green, yellow and purple branches exist in what is America's only underwater monument. On land, a one-mile nature trail spans the course of the island where over 40 species of birds inhabit more than 60 species of trees.

Grassy Point, on St. Croix's south side, *(lower right)* is one of the few shores that does not have sand. Here the green blades of grass are washed by gentle ocean waves.

Saint JOHN

S T. JOHN, smallest and most tranquil of the Virgin Islands, has been called "an emerald set in sparkling sapphire seas." When you see it, you'll know why. Put the beaches of St. John at the top of your "must-see" list. Beaches of sugar-fine sand framed by lush foliage are ideal for lounging beneath these tropical skies. Hawksnest Beach *(left)* rims the north shore and is a favorite among the locals, especially at the height of tourist season.

Cinnamon Bay *(top, right)* is just one of the glistening bays managed by the National Park Service. Two-thirds of St. John is protected by the Park Service, and that includes everything from the neon fish along coral reefs to the campgrounds.

The slow-motion lifestyle of Cruz Bay *(bottom, right)* embraces travelers who want to relax and unwind. The town is so laid back, in fact, that tee shirts and sneakers are about as "formal" as one dresses. Unlike other islands, there's no frenzy to shop, shop, shop! Besides the very modern Mongoose Junction shopping center, there are just a handful of shops. Cruz Bay is just right if all one desires is peace and serenity.

Saint JOHN

T HANKS to a meticulous Park Service, the beaches on St. John are special places indeed. Jet skis and deep draught vessels are prohibited and the shores are free from commercialization.

Trunk Bay *(upper left)*, the island's most popular and surely one of the most stunning, is ideal for swimming. Visitors can lounge in the sun, frolic in the water or picnic beneath the shade of a seagrape tree. Pictures of this smooth, silky beach are often found on post cards.

Farther east lies Maho Bay *(upper right)*, a waterside campground designed to maintain this region's natural beauty...and beautiful it is! This alluring beach-lined bay, bordered by deep green forestry is a sight to treasure. The water here is calm and soothing, excellent for floating on a raft or swimming alongside its resident sea turtles.

Count politicians, celebrities and dignitaries among those who frequent Caneel Bay *(bottom)*. For the utmost in upscale accommodations, the well-to-do make reservations at its luxurious hotels and villas. This elite clientele has access to posh gardens, tennis courts and seven beaches spread over 170 acres. Equally expensive ferries shuttle guests to Charlotte Amalie, St. Thomas and neighboring isles.

Saint JOHN

MORE than 500 acres were teeming with sugarcane at the Annaberg sugar plantation *(lower left)* during the 18th century. Now more than 200 years later, visitors embark on a self-guided tour of its ruins situated on the northern coast of St. John. Roam amid the remnants of slave quarters, windmills and outbuildings of the colonial era. Unlike other ruins on the island, the Annaberg plantation does not have a greathouse because its owner employed overseers to manage operations. While there, make a point to forge to the top for awe-inspiring views of the distant British Virgin Islands.

The Cruz Bay area has some deeply wooded trails that traverse the island. Perhaps one of the more curious sights along the way is that of the Christ of the Caribbean *(top left)*. This giant concrete statue of Jesus towers over the ruins of the Denis Bay Plantation. It was commissioned by a mainlander and erected about 40 years ago. It was donated to the Virgin Island National Park in 1975. The enormous sculpture sets on an area called "Peace Hill" as a symbol of "inner and outer peace."